AF334429

The Rapids

The Rapids

Susan Gillis

Brick Books

Library and Archives Canada Cataloguing in Publication

Gillis, Susan, [date]
       The rapids / Susan Gillis.

Poems.
ISBN 978-1-926829-79-1

I. Title.

PS8563.I5125R36 2012   C811'.54   C2012-903592-0

We acknowledge the Canada Council for the Arts, the Government
of Canada through the Canada Book Fund, and the Ontario Arts
Council for their support of our publishing program.

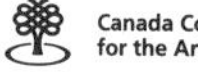

The author photo was taken by Alexandra Pasian.

The book is set in Berthold Wallbaum.

Cover photograph by Max Zerrahn/fStop/Getty Images.

Cover design by Cheryl Dipede.

Design and layout by Alan Siu.

Printed and bound by Sunville Printco Inc.

Brick Books
431 Boler Road, Box 20081
London, Ontario N6K 4G6

www.brickbooks.ca

Contents

Bloodroot

Neruda's Rain

Habitat

Twenty-two Views
of the Lachine Rapids

Bloodroot

The Days

Each day curved, inviting as a bell.
Opened by birdsong and the persistence of surf
or its cousin, wind in the leaves.
Like an open throat, rimmed with the moist lips
of a limitless music.
I climbed in, with my kit of troubled origins.
The sun rose, the sky moved across it
and soon the field grasses became stark.
Nothing was hidden.
All distances were erased,
the crown of the venerable oak across the pond
as tangible as my own heart.
Each day the same: without my noticing,
scope and resonance shrank
till the waves were nearly still
and small disturbances remained small—
By evening everything had softened.
Toads appeared in the garden around the porch.
I became a kind of flower, flush with intention,
brimming, last-ditch. Ready for anything.

Reading *Karenina* on a Chilly Night

Just as I sit down
after clearing the supper things
to wade in the shallows of Vronsky's character

the fridge begins the howl that's grown
louder over the years
like a child grown bigger but never fully up,

drowning the window-rattle
and the plash of rain
under the split in the eavestrough,

gentler sounds, which
now they've been superseded
seem homely and welcome

like household members passing through
coughing and farting and blowing their noses,
affirming the house as a place to lose myself

in the changed and changing
timbre of Anna's mind, the floors
creaking upstairs and joists

popping in new tensions,
the furnace blower harrumphing on
like an old uncle

addressing the company—
what would he say to someone like Anna,
who'd certainly not stop to listen?

Knot

The air was soft in the lane behind houses,
trees and fences uncertain shapes in the dark,
a few windows lit, and high up, the moon
like the pupil of an eye in a photographic negative,
a white constriction in night's speckled iris.

Earlier it had been huge and glowing,
a golden fruit hanging over the skyline.
People stopped, and pointed and gasped,
moved a little apart from each other,
then stood a little closer than before.

We watched it raise its serene, impossible weight
above and slightly westward, slowly becoming
the small knot we'd later be walking home under,
like an illness we walk with, remote, estranged,
like wounded birds.

Quadra Island Suite

1

Small birds flit in the trees,
unconcerned with audience.

I drain my glass,
put off lighting the lamp

then do,
turning the windows black.

2

Moss gleams
on the outcropping over the lake,
the lake a shimmer through alder.

Pines drop their needles
when I'm not looking.

The path is fragrant underfoot.
I follow the fragrance
as it follows me.

3

Past the woodshed
the evening sky
flares over the lake.

4

Silver darts, fish jumping.
My heart, when I say your name.
An osprey circles.

5

Cooling off in the lake
swimming in rings,
each other's eyes our pivot.

6

A hot day
scratching pine needles
from the tight cedar roof-shakes.

Deer flies chase me
to the heart of the lake.

7

To make coffee, roast the beans
then grind them
then throw them into water
then boil up over a flame.

To make a flame, hold a match
to a tent of split cedar.

8

What about all those times
we played like horses
whinnying and tossing our heads?

My spine.
Your braided mane.

9

Cutting salal I cut the heel of my hand.
I was blazing a path up the mountain
to a mossy clearing at the top
that revealed the radiant lake,
the farther mountains,
the curve of sky,
the steep path.

10

That evening a line of quail
came strutting along
the newly opened ground.

By mid-summer new growth
had closed it again.

11

Crossing the frozen lake in tennis shoes.
Look what I can do in my Björns!

12

To split cedar requires cedar.
To split fir is another matter.

Russian Novel

It's windy. The trees are squeaking again.
My dreams are shaking off their details.
All the people have been replaced with leather trunks.
While the trunks are shown the sights—town hall,
main street, marble fountain in the park,
station wall rippling in lake light,
birch nutkins clacking, and so on—the people
are left to stump around on the platform.
It's getting late. For example, that woman
standing near the lake in the white dress.
When will her lover step out of the building?
When will her suitcase come back to her?
Has it become obvious we're running out of time?
Like the birch leaves, the woman sways a little,
her dress rustling. A tiny swoosh, that's all,
then a soft splash, and where she was is nothing.
In the air, nothing.
The torn water closes over itself.
Now a man approaches in mirrored glasses.
Everything breaks apart in their shine.

Stepping Outside the House in Late December

Stepping outside the house at dusk I'm afraid
I'm stepping into another form,
my edges losing their edge, arms shading into the trees,
hair a plume of long grass turned ashen.
Legs loosed from their sockets fly toward the marsh;
the ghost dog chases them.
The chill air that swept by when I opened the door
is not what I thought.
It is the lit and humming *in here*
rushing out of the frame.
All day we stupidly clapped squirrels from the feeders,
preferring the birds.
My tracks begin to fill in,
smudge into the shade that settles on things
like a cloth released over a cage of canaries.
The black horse in the far field whinnies and stamps.
The ridge bristles with trees.
My apprenticeship has begun.

Surge

Wind from the north and the tang astringent, scouring bare fields.

Something in the large trees recalls summer; dormant branches cling
to the sky like tendrils.

Our breath gathers and disperses, small fogs, transient and reassuring.

The immanence of snow, even in a coat shrugged off on a green lawn,
in the muffled sound of a porch door.

Opening and closing in its box of time, the weather slows to admit
a dream, surges when one arrives.

Solstice Night

A blue lake surrounds the house: snow
restored by twilight to a version of its original self,
stippled where wind and animals have crossed,
barred by shadows of trees.
And speaking of trees, shadows fly out from them
like time-traces of late-summer bats, and return.
Everything dampens down.
A sudden stillness—
and the earth's tilt reverses.
Gradually the first stars prick the sky around the moon's pearled curve.
The last of the year's scrap wood is ready for burning.

Also a twilight everything turns from:
stamping our feet on the platform waiting for the train,
lined up on the curb waiting for the bus, blowing on our fingers.
Young men shaking snow from their collars
as they pass through the turnstiles and descend
with everyone else into the tunnels and shopping concourses,
into the wet stink, the grit and slush, blasts of heat and noise
over the hornet-hum of earbuds and ringtones, ignoring
everything, which is a form of love.

Arm in arm a young couple stand in front of a window
brimming with tiny confections. He pulls off her hat—
a sudden stillness—
then breathes into the gold waves of her hair.
And night opens before them like a dinner napkin
or like a carousel starting up, night as a state,
moonless, starless, yet spangling. We're burning
everything we have. We're cheering ourselves on.

On the Station Platform

Everything's frozen, and breaks on contact.
Everyone's staying close to the tracks, not leaning back on the fence.
I eat chocolate for energy but can't taste it.
In this cold everything goes missing.
Near the bridge the steeple is shedding light,
great flakes of it, sloughing into the boughs of surrounding fir.
We're all waiting, stamping our little feet,
printing the map of our waiting into the snow.
There's a sliver of light above the clouds' folds.
The moon has hacked it into the darkening sky.
It used to be thought the liver was the seat of our passions.
If so, there's a crescent-shaped scar in mine
where the moon hacked its way through my body
to open a frozen river.
The train arrives first as broken light—
utterly, utterly silent—
across the trestle bridge, flashing—
then as a screech and roar we press toward,
our hundred exhalations willing open the doors.

The Youth

I've seen a young man
at the edge of the forest.
You may doubt
but I've seen his face,
his gentle eyes
and the calm, clear, easy line of his shoulders.

He wears a hat
of glossy fur
and a dark coat.
I can't see the rest.
But what's in his face—
I see him mornings, and now and then after tea.

He stands quite still
in the tall grass
not watching but looking.
Behind him the trees
are indistinct.
He stands in front of the dark, inscrutable trees.

He never ventures
close to town.
He'd be quite strange.
Wouldn't you like
to see what he sees?
I think there are many who secretly want to see.

And I'm among them.
We want so much
it keeps us from peace.
Quite far out
in felted pelts
we watch for signs of movement in the trees.

Animal

Once I lay down next to a young puma
as if on the lip of a mountain—
oh let's be frank, as if in the eye of some force.
From his resinous gaze light fell in waves of leaves.
More to the point, he had a look that could open a quahog.
The two halves of his chest were silver trout jumping upriver.
His groin, that singular tree,
flared from the twinned fist with its urns of seed.
At his feet, dragonflies clung to witchgrass.
He might have arrived in a rush basket
like a demigod, or bread and wine:
first a breeze stirs.
He gathers himself into himself, rippling.
That still you can feel the air's skin—
then a gust, and the odour of lilies where his body has been.

Let's

say you're the burr
and I'm the soft sweater. Say
I'm the hair, say the hair
in your throat. Your
burr-throat, lion-burr
low in my ear once you growl me down
onto the pillow, let's say
it's a pillow.

Sleep

It opens among the body's dark fruits,
the organs nestled in their niches,
unfurling its heady sweetness
like the wild-rose hedge we walk by in June

stopping for a moment to recall one day in childhood
that had been perfect, though utterly ordinary,
its perfection a quality of light and sound
unlike any other, a plume

so deeply sunk in the body it remained fixed
in a peculiar conjunction of senses, plumped by a breeze.
That night after the blue time of crickets
we saw the lightning bugs, our first, the birth

of the world. So sleep returns to us
now: mother, seducer, priest,
deflating our hot, our fervid concerns,
making way for a softness, a yielding, for

quite unexpectedly a black bear
ambling toward instead of away from us,
the sudden brightness of knowledge,
the room inside us for it.

Saint Jerome in the Wilderness

The animal pauses, roaring; the shaggy fur flares.
Half-hobbled by pain, it lunges on,
tindered in the electrical charge of its progress.
Each slow lift of the hurt paw ripples its haunch.
The man, who has just opened the cloth
in which he carries all he owns—a quill,
a thumb of ink, a book, a small blade—
spreads these things on the ground and stands up
slowly, stands still. Sensation
thorns through him—the first
sweet sink of claws, jubilation
of incisors…. His body is like the thin
willow that grows near the river; his faith,
fully formed in sap and marrow. He does not turn
away, nor does he call out for anything. He holds
his blade like a light, makes his arm a bench.
There is no training for love, only love.
The man waits, then excises the thorn.

Orioles

Yesterday orioles showered the trees with brilliance,
busy as monkeys, cascading at the edge of the woods,
and I forgot to think about my troubles.
Today watching the trees through a thin dampness
I recall a small kindness offered decades ago
by a stranger, kindness I flinched from
like a cat who will not be stroked.
There are objects I still can't look at
without catching my breath, frail chairs
I carry around from childhood, souvenirs
of trips no one remembers, fragments
of torn-down walls. All the same,
"I love the tenacity that still survives in my eyes,"
and the flutter of air on skin that signals a change—

I would like to tell you about the orioles
but a pang in my ribs dissuades me.
How can I open my heart to you
when over and over you show me it's too much—
that, or not enough?

Sanguinaria canadensis

Now we've been apart as long as we were together.
Yet it seems a blink compared to a lifetime,
the span of a dragonfly in the history of dragonflies.
It's not that the years have been lacking in riches—
I've known the copper beech in autumn, the oaks,
hibachi fires that outlast nights of shooting stars,
and later, a fretwork of snow on the grill.
At the far end of winter I watch for the bloodroot,
which returns holding its delicate flower
within cupped leaves whose undersides
are almost morbidly pale, fine-veined and soft
like the skin under parts of our bodies we lift—
Looking at it is like looking at something forbidden;
I was drawn to such apparent modesty then.
Its cut stems yield red juice.
And the name: blood at the root.
It's what I left behind. It's mine.

Into the Storm

Plants! I was happy enough
to select them, but placing them
asked for a certainty that eludes me.

I would lift and move one three centimetres to the left
and down a bit, turn it this way, then that, then dig it up
and try again—

And their vigour! Every morning
I walked through a world slightly altered,
taking a new inventory; each day
trained new tendrils, thinned alstroemeria, clipped back
creeping jenny, coaxed more of the rose up the fence,
trimmed fronds of bronze fennel—

It was worse than having a pet.
And the weeds bounded forward—

I think now what the neighbours called diligence,
the task chosen above all others,
was the garden dividing me.

If I have left my home
it is to watch the ships on the river,

try to learn something.

Sailors sometimes tell of giving
over to a storm, to a force in a storm,
to a moment they knew was the end, only to
wake safely ashore with no memory of passage.

Plucked from one place, set down in another.

They speak of these mysteries in whispers
and call them, justly, miracles.

So what name do we give the force
that propels us *into* the storm?

Something poured from a split-open cloud,
some kind of light that picked me up by the spine
and threw me out of our house.

That was a lifetime ago.

And I'm still wearing the striped sailor's sweater
that happened to be near the door.

〜

If I have moved away from the world
it is because I am helpless against its dazzlements.

What draws scilla out of winter-packed lawns
opens the bud of a windflower
above its frilled collar.

The same force drew me
to a place studded with signs—
shrubs on fire, burning moss, trees
packed with birds giddy with light,
bannering the world to come.

What else could have propelled me
away from our marriage, just as the daffodils
came muscling up through the ground?

The windflower spins for a day
then falls. If I have left the world

it is because I am sick of the world,
its treacherous flowering.

I wanted the ripped-up roof of sky,
peat and stone for a bed.

Bark scraps and needles in the path.

To marry the river,
sprung, and flooding seaward.

Ars Poetica

Between light and reflection, a movement
that nudges your paddle so
for a moment
the canoe is set to slip
·into the dark seam between lake and cliff.
A quickness, a sharp turn, and you're
ashore, nosing a bed of mint.
Between reflection and dream, a feint,
and something's nuzzling your palm,
newly arrived from the rafters, unsummoned,
dawn scampering over the roof.
Between lily and air, the push
in the fist-like bud, knowledge
held without knowing. That's the real.
The shiver of honeycomb built into the door jamb,
a world built in a world, the swarm
calling without cease for your answer,
your movement, the hum.

Open Throttle

The river at cross purposes with itself
plaits and unplaits its several strands,
delta-seeking, asynchronous,
erupting in a welter of ridges and curls
like the face of someone scorned,

like the inept child who lives
inside the other child, working its fingers,
like the first unmappable mountains
and their natal roar. From the lagoon
a flight of ducks rises, arrow-like, oblivious.

The noise is the noise of a jet taking off,
a kitten's purr, the engine of trade,
open throttle to the power stations upstream.
No one can cross the rapids without unnatural force.
They take down freighters like autumn leaves,

like bears swiping at ants, like a kicked wasps' nest.
Beside them even the grandest oaks
are frail, the hunger of babies small.
Standing on rocks at the edge
strakes the body, is good.

What distance this moving and unmoving mass
sets between place and desire.
Its face is the one you could look at forever,
the one you know best and not at all.
Among the bellowing, bucking waves

a few still pools
spangle the sky back to the sky,
wells with invisible walls
beneath whose invisible skin
polyvalent and numberless streams swim.

Neruda's
Rain

The Road to X

Unwrapping our sandwiches—
a small bird rattling.

Deep in the leaf-heart
the last of last year's pomegranates,
dried on the branches,

hanging over the gorge like lanterns.

Spring Pries at Me

Spring makes me sick for coastal cities.
All that burgeoning! Crowds and leaves.
Going for a walk is its own aperitif,
air in the nose like cracked pepper.
Diesel and lilac drift together,
hang around, drift apart.
Such is the nature of ports.
Listen, down by the tracks
seagulls are prying open that rusty box again.

Neruda's Rain

On the edge of the harbour, the traveller's room, you know it
by its worn and patient smell, a delta of grey vibration,
particles suspended, repelling luminosity.

Seeded with private longings
the numberless nameless lodge here,
worm into the city, fill their mouths with dust—

I too press my tongue against the sides of my teeth,
smooth the bedcovers against muffled sensations,
diesel fumes seeping in from the street,

near and far bells ringing in every tower.
In the tumult, running my hands down the sheets,
raising the same dust—

It's like this: open, the window admits more than I can bear.
Closed, it's stifling.
Either way, I can't rest.

Nothing in this room is gracious.
Nothing is rubbed to a loving shine, or dappled,
everything's nicked, marred, bent, chipped, torn,

its light comes not from the window but from floorboards,
not with the gleam of forests but more the slickness of mud:
it has a brackish air, sucking desire,

an air that wants to subsume,
to absorb, swallow, smother, push down.
Nothing wants to be touched.

I am alone here, Pablo, thinking of rain.
Like the dust that swirls around me and seems like me,
alone, and wanting form.

Glimpse: Poetry

Anecdote dressed up with lyric.
All this *feeling*.
The illness of the self writing the illness.

Meanwhile the birds with their juicy songs.
A cardinal has come to the street.
Farther down, snowdrops in the grass.
Hour by hour the frozen river swells.

As for poetry, it lurks,
whatever the poets say—

Blessing

It had been raining for weeks.
Rafts of torn-off artichoke leaves
coursed the flooding lanes.
To look at anything
involved insufferable pain—
wind lacerated the pools,
the ripples worse than poppies in fields.
Birds had stopped singing.
Even the rooster crowed only half his notes.
Though I was desolate,
at least in this I was not alone:
everyone's windows had swollen shut,
and no one remembered lizards.

And then it was the first of May.
Still raining, but patches of sun.
I discovered my boots leaked.
Nico's arms were spread like wings
before I got near enough to hear his greeting.
How could I go with him to the meadow,
I who couldn't bear to be touched?
His kindness flew at me like wind.
My house wasn't cold, yet I was cold.
It wasn't flooding, either,
yet I was flooded with cold.
I could barely close my fingers around a match
let alone somebody else's hand.

Intimacies

On the hotel roof with shawl and aperitif
I'm out of season, it's dusk, droves of cloud
are running into the city from the slopes of the Lefka Ori,
I'm alone and tired of it, tired of breakfast rooms,
of propriety, of folding hunger, etc., back into myself
like the clothes in my suitcase.

Mr. Konstantakis, gentleman, opens the terrace door
and steps in patent slippers into the evening,
nodding hello, showing a little tongue—
once, in the lounge, he helped me find
the satellite channel that carried
the World Cup quarter-finals, something to do
that wasn't walking; I've been walking
a lot in the hills; the steep slopes and rough terrain
know my name.

Mr. Konstantakis, who moves like a tortoise, approaches
and remarks in extremely formal and outmoded French
on the beauty of the evening
and gestures to be invited to sit with me—
you barely have to respond, you know, to these niceties—
mentions rain, and something about *tristesse*,
maybe the way the clouds are closing in, I don't know,
no *Madame*, no *Mademoiselle*, only a kind, intelligent smile
before he embarks on a topic, and the little lizard tongue—
clearly I puzzle him.

I have a story ready concerning a fire
for questions about why I'm travelling alone,
a good one, a real tragedy,
but he waves it away, imagine, without a trace of shame.
Which offends me.

Owner of two hotels, modest exporter of oranges,
Mr. Konstantakis, not peering so much as basking,
tells me I am *aimable*,
a word I don't recognize,
and proposes I dine with him.
He doesn't know I'm really a heap of loose gravel,
only my dress holding me together,
so I do something with my eyes
so he nods and takes his leave.

Glimpse: Zürich Hauptbahnhof

From the train window
I watch my friend:

her green sweater
her bright smile

the station clock above her head

shrinking to a dot—

There's a tightening in my throat.

And a green apple in my rucksack!

The Flower Sellers

On the north side of City Hall, a second city: men and women
milling around in wool sweaters, warming their hands in half-
aprons, twiddling clippers and string, their boots damp and mud-
spackled from the early hours of gathering woodland flowers,
bundled now in tin pails at their feet.

Broad-backed, unbending, a woman in a dark cloth coat fumbles
with a red coin purse before the tight face of a vendor whose left
hand opens and shuts close to her body like a fish's mouth, swims
slowly into the space between her body and her customer with a
need all its own, an itch, an intention she catches and pulls back,
her face unchanging while her hand keeps veering toward what it
wants so sharply it pulls her from sleep and into the woods before
dawn, sand-eyed, bending with secateurs

—except it's not like that. One team gathers, another trims and ties,
a third sells in the square: a romance of efficiency.

The little bunch of flowers gleams as the money changes hands, tiny
blooms pearling stems against blade-shaped leaves. Flaring out in
the background toward the vanishing point, the eastern colonnade.
City officials materialize under its arches like sleek beasts, and
recede. At the far end, a tiny café table and four empty chairs.
Beyond, a shadowy blur, and beyond that, a streak of blue: the first
glimpse of industrial suburb, or a stream at the edge of the woods.

The Auction

I stood on his left, holding up my key.
The auctioneer was a pink-skinned man
in tightly belted trousers and short sleeves
with a microphone clipped to his collar.
He had a way, he entertained the bids
gesturing toward me with his clipboard.

The key was hot in my hand, it glowed.
He droned through the bids in his flowered muumuu—
I wondered about that muumuu,
and the budding rhinoceros horn in his forehead.
I didn't feel very visible up there beside him,
which was both reassuring and disconcerting.

I have felt this kind of erasure
now and then on certain small-pebbled beaches
on my hands and knees sifting the grain-pebbles
for perfect round rice-pearls, the hard
glowing kernels, geology's sleep-dust—

The auctioneer stomped up and down, snorting.
The Scandinavian passenger freighter nodded its head
and bid with crafty eyes; the three-kids-
and-attractive-net-worth husband shot up its arm;
a furnished apartment overlooking the Seine

bent its elbow and flapped its wrist; the membership
in an organization of cheerful people
with adherents all over the world
whose sole mission was to grow
its franchise, jerked its whole eager body
up and down. Yet those bids and others like them

lost to the calm persistent smile
of the small house whose windows look out to the sea
a little walk down from the road,
wild roses hugging its side, and endless
food in the cupboards, whatever I want, whenever.

Intermission

I write because I am
the reincarnation of Aeschylus.
Correction: I *am* Aeschylus.

But I have only two lines. Well,
had. I made them three.
Then I made them two again.

Now I have—
~~seven~~ eight! On summer days I wonder,
what future do I have

as Aeschylus? Outside, the sky
slumps around in its grey caftan
complaining about the weather.

And, sigh, no cobbles, no sparrows
below the window. No artichokes,
no edgy fringes in the wind, no

stoa. And pines? Not for miles.
I have a ticket for tonight's train
but fear I will be late, you know how it is

with trains…. Somewhere
a future is unfolding
and I, Aeschylus, must file, must file a—

Meanwhile the sky loiters,
lowering its judgments.
No consolation. I bet you thought

I was going to say "toga"
back there on line eleven.
I find my best work is done

at higher elevations, where even breathing
is a chore, the air so thin
it might slip away between acts.

The Road to X

This railing:
all that stands between me and the river
at the bottom of the valley.

The pomegranate tree hanging over the gorge,
the bridge we paused on—

The road up to X, the hostel beside the spring,
this balcony.

Material

I'm not sitting on this rooftop under a sky
like a broken mirror, I have never

dug a pit in a backyard, built a fire in it,
I have never eaten that meal.

The roof is not blue, is not supported
with columns of pines. The lake does not leap

when we leap in; we are not, swimming,
so like fish yet not fish. Our bodies do not end

at the air's edge, permeable
as water, which even now as I write

this moment is evaporating.
The day does not settle on our skin,

shadows do not lengthen, certainly
they do not tongue the surfaces of things

as day folds over into darkness—day does not fold
like a child turning in sleep, pulling the blankets up;

there is no child, no sleep; night is not
licking on the lights of the boats in the harbour;

there is no harbour; we do not lean above it at the rail
craning to see what cannot be seen; there is no rail.

Lustral Basin, Knossos

Eight stone steps down, the width of each
a match for depth, a turn, one
last, then the earth floor

where a brazier has burned all night for you,
for your gesture toward it
on your knees.

Not much room in this room.

The embers ask you to lick them, you must
know, deep storehouse of will, you are
flesh, air—

And soaring above, the sky, blue,
blue—

Anchor

On the last day I folded all my clothes,
thin salt-soaked linen and cotton things,
gathered books and maps and bits of stone,

clay shards, postcards I'd never sent,
sandals, bunches of herbs, a bag of giant beans,
bracelets, perfumed oil, a lump of pumice;

wrapped in a towel the early morning shimmer
of fish in crates on the quay, the full noon reek
of nets heaped up, the suck of clams,

the south wind with its grit and flapping sheets
and plastic bags and eucalyptus fronds; shoved in
the loud neighbour and the kind neighbour and the sombre butcher,

his laughing son and the pickle-nosed lame man and the foreign widow
and the young men on scooters and the young women tossing their hair
and the children miming them and those playing with sticks in the creek,

the donkey bray, the urgent farmer who'd lost his mule,
the blue blue blue of his shirt, the care in his voice, "Me mule-y,
me mule-y, *echete thee to moulari mou?*" and the mule,

the evening sky accordioning into red after our death-walk across the cliff,
the wild herbs laced with carrion stink from the rocks below,
your steady voice and one foot after the other across the invisible

ledge my only anchor, that and the tiny ship in the harbour,
please be watching, surely as long as we're seen we're safe,
here, real—I closed the suitcase, squeezed the zipper shut.

Because there is time, I go down to the shore.
The sand is white, the waves leave white
traces they lap away again.

I peer at the white sand, pick out a shell
as tiny as the grit under my fingernail.
And pick another, and another, and another,

casting aside any bigger than dust,
filling a wrinkle in my palm with every shade
of white, every perfect, irregular form,

on hands and knees seeing so far into the sand
it seems I'm seeing through a curtain of heaven
into heaven, pushing my fingers through it,

then my arm, then my shoulder, my head, my whole body,
as though I am swimming back,
as though I can breathe sand

and everything shines: there's never been any other
than this now: the manifold earth,
the constant, replenishing sea.

Habitat

Habitat 67

Like the yellow poplar leaves blown onto the walkway on the tenth
floor, blown nine floors above the topmost branches during the ride
up from the car park in the elevator,

like the bronze oak leaves hanging on through first frost, through
February, through storms, only pushed off by buds.

We Stand Here Looking

Like many, I see it first from the river,
improbable, arbitrary-seeming.
Crannied as a sea stack, nest-
populated, engineered by glaciation,
thermal flux, earth-accident.

Slowly the jags resolve themselves
into made things on a made shore,
blocks gripped by a central core,
each with a sweeping view of partial
things: beyond the river, the flood

plain and rising hills, or the city
roads and buildings and the port.
Here is Safdie, stacking the future
in Mediterranean terrace houses
craned onto fill in a cold Canadian river.

A good maker inhabits the material.
We stand here looking.
Come, the building says
with terrible urgency.
Come lie down in my rooms.

Entry

I turn the key; my free hand swallows the handle.
The door pivots, ushers me in.
The floors click softly, sensing me.
I'm entering the rooms of a woman yet to be invented,
rooms so airy they murmur.
Before it enters, light crosses the river,
but I'm not looking at it.
I'm looking at its un-shy movement, its wavery sheen,
its slip and slide and ghosting on the walls.
When I move through the rooms it brushes me
and I shimmer a little.
It's like a voice, or the organs of the body.
Whatever I touch—the back of a chair, a hibiscus leaf—
incarnates into something I don't yet know.
When I say the rooms are empty, I don't mean empty of things.

Two Birches

The oak floor remembers our first waking,
our padding across it to the terrace doors,

the pungency of leaf mould leaking in
over the threshold. Rising from the port,

river sludge and the ships' sharp fuels.
In such sharpness the two birches from childhood

branch out as if through liquid and solid light,
the sky foliate and dangling. Inscribed in their bark,

the forest romance: expeditions downriver
to the confluence, drinking the cold

twig syrup. Going barefoot outside
for more than a few minutes

even at the height of summer
is a dream. We build temples to it.

Elevation

In noon light the south elevation
resembles a nautilus in cross-section,
rooms dangled around the plumb line
ganged up in clusters; or a grain of sand
barnacled, limed, cemented

into stone, boiler-lunged; or
a crenellation left in a seabed
when the sea shrank away—I can't
order the plans into rooms, they show a door
to a terrace court

but when I walk through
it's into somebody's swimming pool.
Up the left lane and down the right
around a boulevard of tropical plants
under steel trusses and glass and ruthless light

a stranger is swimming. I want to know
what happened. "A corridor runs between,"
she says. But does it divide or join? "Please,"
she adds, nodding toward the springboard,
and I climb on, for this is a living room.

Screen Door

On days of very low cloud, more hanging mist than cloud,
nets of it, rags, vapour batting,

go out on the balcony, you can stand right in it.
Just open the screen and step out.
Hey there, you with your feet in the clouds.

That's what I like best about the balcony,
just standing there, floating almost, the edge of something
on your skin, the fleece of weather.

You can touch the tips of the mountain ash
that arcs over the lawn, twizzle its leaves,
be a conduit between the tree and the house. Zing!
It stands my hair on end almost.

Inside, the floor is swaying in the breeze.

Glimpse: Dust

Best not to think about the ground too much.
Think air, sky, the creatures that move through it:
insects, birds, invisible things, dust

if dust is a creature—

A Good Plan

But let me go back
further. We began to think
about a house, a building,
simply to own our debt.
Scale mattered; small

was beautiful. We thought:
smallest monster house
in the city—five rooms
above a basement,
circling a chimney,

without a hall. Think
chambered nautilus.
It was a good plan.
Two hearths
opened from the centre,

a garden strip
wound around the foundation,
fecund and heat-generating.
Ourselves inside, tiny,
looking up.

Saint Jerome in His Study

He chose the smallest room, drew open
windows, opened books. Rain-light
pours in but not the rain itself,

night is coming on but the bread and cheese
remain untouched. Behind him, also untouched,
the sumptuous divan. Below, on the river,

ships bear down, shuddering sideways toward
the pier; stacks of containers rise in the yards
like civic housing projects. The air cracks

with storm and communications. The saint
does not mind the lack of a bowl of crocuses.
He is kneeling at a bench, nib in hand.

The lion, squatting, lifts its paw as though
begging for a romp in the rain—only then do we see
he is not holding a pen but a blade, ready

to prise out the thorn. What does it mean
to be wild? His gaze is drawn past the lion
to a corner of the room we aren't shown.

Saint Jerome in the Park

Having wandered onto the trail because it led uphill,
having swallowed a decaf grande non-fat latte and taken up walking again,
having approached a quiet grove near parking and concessions
and lain down

under a not especially wholesome oak, one of few,
not because of its wide, authoritative trunk
nor the comforting, vaguely hand-like shape of its leaves
but quite by chance, or, as he might say to himself
if he allowed explanations, drawn here
all unwitting while thinking
of something else, say the opacity of purpose,
by inspiration, the God-breath, he lies here still

in his centuries-old dirty linen robe and twine sandals,
ropey legs sticking out, darkened by leaf-mash and years
spent stumbling around the city's many dead ends
searching the port and the neighbourhoods
for entrances to the wild, his wire-thin arms
twitching, like a creature the birds have laid out,
an effigy of himself, dreaming the end of fire.

In the distance, the foothills of another country.
Nearer, the river. Nearer still, the buildings.
Now the animals, watching.

A Funny Arrangement

Even looking back is a motion forward.
Think of O., closing the future in a glance
over his shoulder at E.—was it the left,
the heart drawing the head too far?
I could sip wine all winter on this balcony
if the weather allowed, wallowing
in looking back to anything, the day we married
say, or further, to the moment we met—people
said they could see it, all parts of my life
landing in alignment; I was a cat
coming down from a tree. What I had seen

up there was not the world but a funny
arrangement of shapes. Nor could I have seen
myself on this tipsy balcony, straining to see
upstream toward the Lachine Rapids
that stranded early explorers in Montreal.

View with Umbrellas

When did it happen, the day's light leaning
so low nothing has dimension anymore?
Autumn has slipped by—suddenly the walk
is a ukiyo-e print, red and yellow
leaves against the wet ground, thin
lines a few figures hurry through
huddled under umbrellas—predictable, ubiquitous
umbrellas, archetypal. One of them
has just blown inside out, revealing
its frail frame, while above, brittle trees
claw the sky. Birds take shelter
under shrubs. To venture out—for milk,
eggs, fruits-and-veg—means thinning to a smudge,
slipping smoke-like underneath the door.

Still Standing in Front of the Door

Thirty years collapse in the hot stench of concrete
to a rainy afternoon in a stairwell somewhere.
He was tall and blond, with hands like racehorses.
I was out of my neighbourhood.
Concrete stays damp for days after rain,
carries the resin of weather in its pores.
And history is no different: it sets,
then somebody knocks away the forms.
Coarse and raffish unexpected visitor
sprawling in the Barcalounger of my nose,
are you telling me I haven't forgotten a few things
after all? The sweet little ring or necklace
or whatever it was he gave me that Christmas? His name?
An hour or so, lodged in me like a clot.
He was bony and tall, and very blond,
and his hands were thoroughbreds. Tell me,
how long did you say you were planning on hanging around?

Birthday

The ships are little fires on the river, candles
you can't blow out. Breath
only has so much power, after
all, like luck. Mostly our lives
flow along like skeins of water in the river,
side by side much of the way, mixing a bit
close to the islands. Year after year
comes and goes, and we just go on
notching the doorposts with our little hatchets.
Come then, husband, stranger.
The city is decked out, the port is on fire.
We are waiting for you
to make your wish.

River

Today wind is driving the snow horizontal.
The window is flocked with cryoplankton
intently building their bronchiole-edged cities,
impervious to the coming thaw.
Through the window the shape of the bridge
is not the shape of the bridge.
My father taught me how to carry a coffee:
just look where you're going, he said,
not down at the cup. It's been
good advice. And, about my *volte-face*—
you're not wrong to call it that.
You know the story of the night bird
and its pebble-throated song?
As it sang, its breast filled with stones.
Its song became a river of stones
which the bird felt as pleasure.
Clear-eyed friend, I found myself
in a city more unlike my own
than I could bear.
I came here to look at the river.

Twenty-two
Views of the
Lachine Rapids

Spring Storm

Yesterday I burned the toast
so I went down to the rapids.
It was not a bright morning.
Close to shore a small twig
spun on an eddy. The eddy
was frilled like a doily, and seethed.
The twig was helpless to go anywhere
except around and around.
On the horizon plumes of smoke
rose like poplar trees. There was
the sun, punched into the sky
like the sky's navel. The river,
pricked and lifted by windhooks.
Mist puffing up, the sky black then white.
Columns of air I could have walked
like pathways to waiting jets,
walked into the skyhold. I'm telling you:
then the river reared up like a dragon,
scales flapping; the sun, smoke,
the far faint islands, all
collapsed in the froth of its lashing.
I had never been so small,
atomic. I was tossed. I have to
say "maelstrom." I wanted out.
I wanted time to turn back.
When I felt the ground again I was
shaking. It seemed I could reach
in any direction and touch the opposite
shore, the islands, the mist and smoke.
The gaps among things had closed.
I'm telling you this because I have not
been able to separate them, and now
all wounds are nothing, are blips,
leaf-loss. Nothing resists.
When I leave, understand, I will not be gone.

View with Aftermath of Storm

Shorn branches, crushed shrubs, saplings doubled over,
the great willow: downed like a stalk of asparagus,
storm-laid on the wreckage of its falling.
What light there is seems to emanate from its core,
the raw inner fibres splintered and exposed
like secret and shameful cravings.
Where I touch, the cells recoil.
Already the edges are withering,
calling silently to the young leaves, still green and buoyant.
In the unsettled sky a few birds hover—three, maybe a fourth.
The rapids, a darker darkness, are sutured with foam.

View with Cameos

Above the calm, immaculate air
a more restless, nervous air accumulates,
snarling invisible strands of sky,
lashing tree limbs, startling birds, I know it
by the swishing sound just discernable
over the river's racket. Not that it
touches me, strolling the gravel path
down low by the river, if by *touch*
we mean on the skin, and if by *skin*
we agree to exclude the eardrum.
Little tympanum, I love what you give me
in a typical day, winds I'd otherwise miss
except for chill or eye, birds secreted in cedar.
And who alert to arrivals hasn't heard a shadow?
This spring the standing waves push higher than ever,
glassy-skinned, vociferous.
All this rushing around the river.
The eddies gleam like rubbed shell,
each the silhouette of another
dear friend lost or departed, carved in relief
like our lives, full of noisy intent
and vortical pull.

View with Mourning Couple

Approaching over the curved footbridge on a perfectly ordinary
late spring day, families out for walks, hair loose, trees leafy
and tangled, recognizable as trees, daubs of white way out on
the rapids...

Forsythia. Or, a yellow jacket caught in the shrubs, in shreds.

A heron on shore, or a rusty buggy.

A rock in the grass, or a small creature curled in torment.

Torment, or counting to a hundred.

The rest of the children running around in the bushes and
long grass, hiding like Easter eggs, their shiny wrappers and
soft chocolatey smell.

Honeycomb of light, the fieldstone path. Heels rapping.

A man and a woman in cloth coats, their hair black and shining,
out for a stroll, pushing a coffin, a coroner's photo fixed to the
top: a young man lying in a twisted repose, darkness at the
gunshot wound, a building, night, the faint inadequate light.

At the end of the path, rocks and river spume.

Droplets of water, or midges' wings.

Glimpse: Unimaginable

The top of the house coming off, that's what woke us, helicopters lowering onto the white X on the hospital roof just up the hill, open throttle, their inconceivable cargo. Shook us from dreaming, and we were suddenly small, impossibly small platelets, groping in the darkness that geysers out of everything—

View at Dusk

Tonight the river is green and radiant with forging.
I could believe in an earlier us, fish with small limbs
racing toward the estuary, leaping in the spring tide,
Piscis ludens splashing at the shore.
The currents carving the river a wider bed.
New sea vegetables springing up at the mouth.
Just a few nights ago the moon was new.
Even over the city the sky was dark enough to see stars,
and Mars appeared, our precursor, oracle
of city shambles, blood-blasted desert, drought.
I've been watching the satellite news.
First, "water was found."
Then "horizons of salt rose in our eyes, far out in the abyss
where a mountain was forming—"
Dear friend, for weeks it's been too hot to do anything.
The world is calling out for the world
and all the fish are making for the same green state—

View with Memling's *Portrait of a Young Man*

Despite his youth, he appears to be a man of some importance, perhaps a shipping scion visiting the port. The unusual seven-eighths view draws our attention to the broad shoulders, the well-cut coat, the horn-tipped string at his collar. His hair is dressed in the Italian fashion of some years earlier: the coarse curls tamed, rolled over his brow and flowing well below his ears. Time has eroded the bloom from his cheeks, yet his lips retain their cherubic smile, the hair the only evidence of the tiger springing inside him. Behind him the fields fall away. From a copse of trees over his left shoulder, the river rises and crosses behind his neck. The sky is a streak of blue. A squall of geese clusters below the horizon. The placid-seeming river carries delicate white shimmers of what we take for swans.

Tag Day

Cooling down after the final stretch to Laprairie Basin
the rapids slow to ripple, veer around the spit
into a shallow pool and rustle of shoreline willows
at the protected nesting ground.
Knee-deep around the projecting rocks
men in shiny hipwaders are doing a slow ballet
with nets and plastic boxes and their arms,
scooping and sieving and tagging
just out of view of the young couple pushing a stroller
along the gravelled path above, past *Acer saccharinum*,
around *Rosa rugosa*, beyond the plaque that diagrams
the migrating birds they might have seen.
On shore a group of friends is eating sandwiches.
One of the men in the shallows shouts
and lifts a flashing thing to his chest, holds it
as he would an injured child. Slick, shuddering,
it torques; he teeters—
a stillness of current and weather—
and someone staples a tag below the dorsal fin:
Esox lucius, the northern pike, caught, counted, released.

Summer Rain

Sudden rain—the shallows criss-crossed
like snake-back, stippled in the darting light.
I had been trying to measure
how far into the water I could see
before deflection obscured everything.
Taking the measure of loss
is like trying to count rocks in the river:
you know they are there
because you see them, and you feel
if you hold still long enough
you could register each one, but the current
keeps breaking the pattern and you lose
count you can't tell where.
The rain is a reminder.
I'm waiting for the dog I know
will show up soon, snuffling the river smells
with eager joy, and the tall young man
who's bound to follow
with an easy stride and a fine camber to his hips—

View with Teenage Girl

The blue knit top with scooped-out neck
and column of gleaming buttons a boy could look at
very, very closely, and say in a hoarse jokey voice
How about I take a look at those buttons,

and after an age that no sound fills
but a soft drumming in her ears
she would say *So,*
you look with your hands do you.

That's the summer she learns about
two kinds of boy, one who replies
Mm-hmm, sure do, and moves easily on,
having basically been walked

and another, who, missing a beat,
feels sharply ashamed
as though he's been caught stealing
so instantly hates her, hates all girls,

even his mother, who appears for a ghastly second
to actually be a girl, but that passes
and he gathers himself
and manages a second try—

and she loves him a little for being not simple,

for his slight, incomprehensible pause,

that small eddy in his excitement
she finds so tender

as it pulls her into the current
she has no real clue underlies it.

Picnic

They choose a spot—how?
The ground is level, the trees far off by the shore.
Some arrangement of molecules presents itself

and the woman bends, spreads a blanket.
The man, sitting now, hands her things from the basket

and calls to the children, who are running giddy ant-patterns
in the space between the blanket and the trees.
The river seems almost idle, its noise

soft as paper towels being crushed.
Now the adults get up
and they and the children swarm together awhile

before collapsing onto the blanket, their centre, their portable hearth
where they lean on elbows and hips

catching the passage of day into evening in their hollows.
Long after they leave, it will stay light, if only faintly,
and the grass sprightly and green.

Autumn Migration

A sudden flapping—
and the island of ducks lifts,
angles over the spit, thins to a line
that veers across the rapids, heading south.
The lagoon they leave hardly shivers, its lit skin
overlaid with a film of cloud and willow,
presence then absence then presence
as we cross the short bridge.
A twig releases a leaf.
The water holds it.

View with Portrait of Frida Kahlo

November, the avenues bare.

Wind like sheets of steel, shore willows hard against it.

Equipment in the sky: cloud, sun, wind,
a few birds hanging on.

The river bucks like that last drink, the one you shouldn't have had,
the drone, pitch, clang, crash, and slam of it.

Pressure from above and below.
Air and obstruction, constriction, gradient, flow.

Walking or standing, it's the same thing.

Out there the waves are assembling the face of Frida Kahlo:
her surging brow, the fathomless eyes, the dark fathoms around them,
quick down-strokes either side of the nose, the sweet

flourish that curls to the nostrils, those racing caverns, not to mention
the dent above the flush of mouth, the knife edge
of closed lips, the tiny cleft in her chin.
The whole vast tropic

bursting with white flowers.

A line of froth slashes her brow.
Go back to bed, the river says.

The wind abates, but her features persist.

Funny way to show you what you need.

Advancing Storm

Mist billows up, and from the east
columns of hawk-wind advance on the river.
Their thousand talons hook and pin it to the racing sky.
The river's clipped skin, froth-peaks.

Meanwhile the shrubs, the avenues of willow,
pathways of flattened snow—our pathways—
fill with cloud. The sun, bilious yellow,
is the sky's eastern navel. For a moment

between islands an aperture opens: snow
breaks into prism, the river bellows its now.

Mid-Winter Dragon

Even frozen they are impassable, dragon
rapids, the river caught in its own thrashing.
Chop and foam hardened to blocks, cracked,
splintered, broken, roughed up, knocked around

and cleaved again—winter of discontent.
Even the bells, pealing across the city,
shearing frost from the morning's stillness,
shaking the bell-sound awake in me,

can't blast the seized rapids:
they smash even the ringing air.

View, Late Winter from the Edge of the Spit, Midpoint

Through the screen of leafless willows the rapids appear almost calm, bulging slightly beneath the water's skin. The patchy clouds in the fragment of sky visible through the branches release parcels of light that fall on the waves and take their shape. On the shoreline, directly in front of the larger willow, a flat, pearled pool shines, nearly as dark as the rocks amongst which it forms. Beyond the pool, farther out, a nest of silver snakes appears to writhe at one end of a vortex shaped as a shallow bowl. The brilliance of the vortex suggests a sun, tailed by fiery rays that tangle and lash in a dizzying snarl. From this solarity's distant edge, a path of light broken into what might be stepping stones leads to a silvery field dark with blossoms. Around the field the river churns dully away to the horizon, where a mottled wedge of darkness stands for the trees of the distant shore. All of this is overlaid by the black twisting fingers of the willow that dominates the foreground. At its base, easily taken at first for a clutch of mushrooms, a small leather shoe kicks through a pile of decaying leaves.

Retreating Ice

Count on it, every spring
you will find the river again.

Rocks at the edge will re-emerge
like loaves of bread salvaged from your freezer.

Our genial host will press the river into taking off its hat and coat,
just as the guileless stranger in the story
is persuaded again and again to take off his hat and coat—

Between the sun and the others, it's clear who'll win.

If you look into the water you'll see the young fry swarm
newly hatched from their jelly, and mudpuppies lurking by their
        broods.
All manner of things will come near
if you stay very still.

The plaintive sound you hear vibrating through the valley
strafing your core if you let it,
that's the anguish of departure.

I've been in retreat a long time, shrinking back, leaving
farmland, rivers, new creatures in new habitats—

But you, how could you lose your place in the world,
when the world so persistently calls you?

Picnic

The grass springs back, erasing our path.
We sit on one shore looking across at the other,
cups and bowls and a plate of tomatoes beside us.
Hard by, the dark bead of a gull's eye, sturdily advancing.
The white mist of the rapids shines as it disperses, continuously,
the opposite of rain. The distant islands a haze of pine.
The river a trench we can't cross.
What can we say we haven't said a thousand times?
Heat pearls our skin.
We say it anyway.

View at Dawn

I stood in the anteroom,
a cool, unembellished place,
waiting for a performance or an exam,
voices like strands of crystal beads,
the air crackling like a sweater coming off,
everyone's hair a little more full

and when it dawned on me you weren't
just late, the room dimmed
and its talk dimmed and softened.
I turned to the picture window
that gave a view of the western sky.
The pale moon was high and almost full

and as I stood, an arc appeared on the horizon:
rising fast, filling the field, becoming an orb
so huge and close I started back

as though it had bumped my eyes.
It rose and hung in the zenith of its orbit.
Vapours swirled around it in shifting hues.
Rivers and fields stretched beyond it infinitely,
bending into their own vanishing.
Nothing was dark anymore.

Behind me the room had filled with song.
I turned,
and all the people had sprouted leaves
and were shaking them.

The Flower Sellers, Remix

I woke under the arches of City Hall to the din of men and women
in ravelled sweaters hawking flowers they get from the woods
and keep in tin pails. They go into the woods with cutters before
sunrise. The bunches are small and tied with blue string. The
women who buy them wear cloth coats and count their change.
None of the fur ladies go near them. I turned the corner into
another yard, bummed a coffee outside a busy café. The sidewalk
bricks are very red. If the hawkers are still there when I'm done
I might get a bunch, if I can scrape up the means I will, if scare
up I mean

> ~~*soap*~~
> ~~*an orange*~~
> ~~*chocolate biscuits*~~
> ~~*cherry jam*~~
> ~~*room*~~
> *small bunch lily of the valley*

Glimpse: Sufficiency

When we are young we brush dirt from our knees
and go on playing, all capacity.

Later the same gesture repeated idly in a stadium seat,
brushing cloth over our knees, brings a blindness of grief.
We are sitting with strangers. The man at our side
is not the one we married with dreams of orchards,
and he too suffers.

Even at night light furnishes the sky, the trees.
The trick is finding a place dark enough to see it—

View at Dusk

Across the rapids a blue orb floats on a leggy plinth
above the line of trees that marks the edge of the seaway.
Shipping cranes paused for the day
point northeast and southwest toward industry.
What goes on over there, see, is that the channel floods,
and a ship is lifted thirty feet closer to home. Upstream

the river widens to lake, and bliss
is a matter of knots and pinging halyards,
rpm of a speedboat, young riders churning wake.
Oiled arms that pull at oars.
Like what happens in the locks, it's beyond what I can see.

And downstream, sediment gathers
as the river courses toward the gulf.
Tides and porpoises appear.
I've slept and woken in a small room at the edge of this transition,
clarified by estuarial roar—

Except for the river, everything races dusk
to the point beyond the bridge
where the sun, shrunk to a speck, funnels
into itself, siphoning us of form,

the western sky agleam, flocked
with shapes of what we were
and what we will become.

Notes and Acknowledgements

The line quoted in "Orioles" is from Pablo Neruda's "Sonata and Destructions" published in *Residence on Earth*, translated by Donald D. Walsh. "Neruda's Rain" borrows its closing lines, with variations, from "The Dawn's Debility" in the same volume.

The poems in the third section pay tribute to Habitat 67, Moshe Safdie's architectural icon in Montreal. "Habitat 67" nods at Richmond Lattimore's translation of Sappho 105a, 105c (Lattimore #8), from his *Greek Lyrics.* "Saint Jerome in His Study" transposes the scene depicted in Albrecht Dürer's 1514 engraving of the same title to an interior in Habitat 67.

The quoted lines in "View at Dusk" are from Paul Celan's "Behind the charcoal surfaces of sleep—" published in *Glottal Stop: 101 Poems*, translated by Nikolai Popov and Heather McHugh. The portrait by Hans Memling referred to in "View with Memling's *Portait of a Young Man*" hangs in the Montreal Museum of Fine Arts/Musée des beaux-arts de Montréal. Environment Canada's St. Lawrence Centre provided information on the structure, biology, and history of the river and the rapids at Lachine.

The term "Björns" in "Quadra Island Suite" refers to a model of tennis shoe endorsed by Björn Borg. This poem is for Robert Kidd. "View with Mourning Couple" is dedicated to Luis and Sandra Merino.

Poems from this book first appeared, sometimes in different versions, in *The Antigonish Review, Arc, Branch, CV2, Encore, The Fiddlehead, The Literary Review of Canada, The Malahat Review, Matrix, The New Quarterly, Poetry Quebec, sunday @ 6 mag*, on the Parliamentary Poet Laureate's Poetry Webpage, on CBC Radio, and in the *Montreal Gazette*. My thanks to the editors and instigators of these publications.

Warm thanks to Andrew Steeves, Gary Dunfield, and the team
at Gaspereau Press, who published the limited-edition chapbook
Twenty Views of the Lachine Rapids (Gaspereau Press, 2012), which
includes many of the poems in the fourth section, some in slightly
different versions.

Grants from the Canada Council for the Arts and the Conseil des
arts et des lettres du Québec helped in the development of this
manuscript. I am grateful to these organizations for their continuing
support of writers and the literary arts.

Choruses of thanks to my editor John Barton for his care and
persistence, and to Barry Dempster, Kitty Lewis, Alayna Munce,
Cheryl Dipede, and the whole excellent team at Brick.

Heartfelt thanks to the friends and readers whose conversation
enriches these pages.

This book is for John Steffler.

Susan Gillis has lived on the east and west coasts of Canada. Poet, teacher, and member of the poetry collective Yoko's Dogs, she divides her time between Montreal and the lake country of Ontario. *The Rapids* is her third book.